Useni Eugene Perkins
Illustrated by Laura Freeman

Special book excerpts or customized printing can also be created to fit specific needs.
For details, write or call the Just Us Books special sales office.
P.O. Box 5306, East Orange, New Jersey 07019 973.672.7701
Just Us Books and the Just Us Books logo are trademarks of Just Us Books, Inc.
ISBN: 978-0-940975-86-6

Printed in United States of America
10 9 8 7 6 5 4 3 2 1

Kwame Nkrumah stood stately, a traditional Northern smock on his slender, ebony body.

Thousands of Ghanaians and dignitaries from other countries filled the Polo Grounds in Accra on the humid night of March 6, 1957.

They gathered to hear Prime Minister Nkrumah announce the Gold Coast's independence from many years of British rule.

At the stroke of midnight, while the moon shone brightly, the British Union Jack was lowered.

The tricolored flag of Ghana, with the black lodestar of African freedom at its center, was raised. The new flag swayed gently in the breeze.

In a jubilant voice, Kwame Nkrumah declared Ghana a sovereign nation.

*"At long last, the battle has ended!
And thus Ghana, your beloved country,
s free forever!"*

Independence for Ghana did not come without years of struggle by the Ghanaian people.

And the courage of people like Kwame Nkrumah, who were determined to free their homeland from the British.

Nkrumah's vision for a free Ghana began when he was a student at Achimota College in Accra. There he met Dr. Kwegyir Aggrey, who introduced him to Pan-Africanism, the idea that people of African heritage have common interests and should be unified.

Nkrumah excelled in his studies and earned a reputation as a persuasive speaker. He became a teacher and decided to continue his education in the United States.

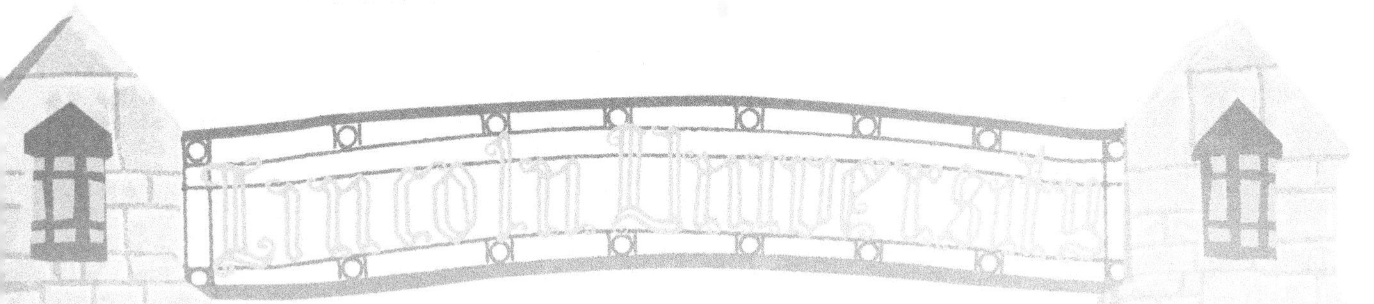

In 1935, Nkrumah enrolled at Lincoln University, a historically Black institution in Pennsylvania. He earned a degree in Sociology then studied at the University of Pennsylvania, where he received degrees in Theology and Education.

Nkrumah began to teach at Lincoln. He also edited a newspaper called the *African Interpreter.*

Those achievements earned him many invitations to speak at Black churches. His favorite church was Abyssinian Baptist in Harlem, pastored by Reverend Adam Clayton Powell, Jr.

Nkrumah remained in the United States for ten years. He spoke at street rallies, political meetings and with Black leaders. He discovered that Black people in the United States and in his native Gold Coast shared a common struggle. Both were being denied their basic human rights. He knew this was happening other places where Black people lived, too.

He was determined to do something about it.

In 1945, Nkrumah went to Manchester, England where he helped to organize the Fifth Pan African Congress.

He met with other African and international leaders including Jomo Kenyatta, W.E.B. DuBois, and C.L.R. James who were fighting for independence in Africa.

They believed in self-rule. One of their slogans was "Africa for the Africans!"

Members of a new organization, United Gold Coast Convention, heard about Nkrumah's leadership and wanted him to assist them in fighting for the rights of the people of the Gold Coast.

Nkrumah was inspired. Other leaders encouraged him to return to his home-land to help lead the fight.

CPP
FREEDOM
Forward Ever, Backward Never

Nkrumah became secretary of the UGCC and traveled throughout all the regions of the Gold Coast to establish local chapters.

Thousands came to hear him speak powerful words about freedom, justice and self-government.

Eventually, Nkrumah and members of the UGCC began to disagree over the tactics that should be used to fight for independence. The UGCC wanted to move slowly. Nkrumah believed the people could not wait.

So he formed another organization, the Convention People's Party. He was so successful, the British began to see him as a threat to their authority.

The British authorities accused Nkrumah of inciting riots. In 1950, he was arrested for his political activities and put in Accra's James Fort prison. But he continued to lead the CPP movement from his jail cell.

When the British government finally called for an election that allowed Black people to participate in the government, CPP won a majority of the seats. Nkrumah won a seat, too.

When Nkrumah was released from prison he was asked to form and lead a new government.

At first, he was reluctant. But he accepted the position as Prime Minister knowing that much still needed to be done to achieve true independence for his people.

Nkrumah helped to write a new constitution for his country. It would serve as the framework for his midnight speech for independence.

Kwame Nkrumah continued his speech.

"And yet again, I want to take the opportunity to thank the people, the youth, the farmers, the women, who have so nobly fought and won the battle.

Also, I want to thank the valiant ex-servicemen who have cooperated with me in this mighty task of freeing our country from foreign rule and imperialism."

Nkrumah believed that no African country should be under the rule of Europeans.

In closing, he shared his vision for all other African nations that had been colonized by European countries.

"Our independence is meaningless unless it is linked up with the total liberation of Africa."

After a moment of silence, the band played the National Anthem of Ghana.

Kwame Nkrumah left the Polo Grounds with a sense of pride that Ghana was now a free nation. And the thunderous cheers of the people echoed in the night.

AUTHOR'S NOTE

During his life—as a student, an educator and a statesman, Kwame Nkrumah gave many speeches, to gatherings of all sizes. But his most impressive speech of all was delivered on March 6, 1957 in front of an audience of hundreds of thousands.

For years, Nkrumah's powerful and passionate words have been recited by school children and adults alike. Parts of his Independence Day speech have been quoted during Ghana's annual Independence Day celebrations just as Dr. Martin Luther King Jr.'s famous "I Have a Dream" speech is often quoted in the United States.

I was inspired to write a book about Kwame Nkrumah and his Midnight Speech for Independence after one of my early visits to Ghana. Nkrumah's words are famous all over the continent of Africa and the world because they motivated and inspired hundreds of freedom fighters and emerging nations on the world's second largest continent. In a speech of less than seven minutes, Nkrumah was able to express fierce pride in his country and a deep respect for wisdom and the rich cultural heritage which had been passed down by his ancestors. It also conveyed his faith in the people of Ghana and confidence in their ability to govern themselves as a free and independent nation.

I wanted to write about the significance of not only Nkrumah's speech but also the tremendous role that he had in shaping a vision and philosophy of the modern Republic of Ghana. What started out as a poem praising an independence day speech gradually developed into a picture book about Kwame Nkrumah and the struggle for his country's independence. Laura Freeman added even deeper layers of meaning to this story by beautifully weaving Adkinkra symbols into all of the illustrations. These symbols, which are acknowledged by most ethnic groups in Ghana, are primarily indigenous to the Asante people. They symbolize traditional proverbs, wisdom and guiding principles that the people of Ghana have embraced as part of their national identity. Laura's artistic rendering of the story is simply captivating.

Kwame Nkrumah was the first Prime Minister and first elected President of the Republic of Ghana. Born in 1909 and raised in the Asante region of his country, in 1957 he helped to establish Ghana (formerly known as the Gold Coast) as the first sub-Saharan country in Africa to gain independence from the colonial power of Great Britain. He served as Ghana's president from 1961 to 1966 and was also a principal leader of the Pan-African movement until his death in 1972.

Educated in Ghana, the United States, and Great Britain, his studies included philosophy, education, government and theology. He also studied African culture and history. Kwame Nkrumah was heavily influenced by the ideas of Black intellectuals and leaders such as W.E.B. DuBois, Marcus Garvey, George Padmore and C.L.R. James and he merged many of these ideas into his ideology and philosophy of Pan-Africanism.

Nkrumah's Midnight Speech for Independence and celebrations surrounding it were attended by dignitaries from around the world including Dr. Martin Luther King, Jr., Coretta Scott King, A. Philip Randolph, Congressman Adam Clayton Powell, Jr., Nobel Peace Prize winner Ralphe Bunche, Great Britain's Duchess of Kent and then-Vice President of the United States, Richard Nixon.

The Midnight Speech for Independence is considered an important milestone in the struggle for self-rule and independence in Africa and beyond.

The powerful words of this speech still resonate with each Independence Day celebration.

"And thus, Ghana, your beloved country, is free forever! . . . Our independence is meaningless unless it is linked up with the total liberation of Africa."

—Useni Eugene Perkins

ADINKRA SYMBOLS and Their Meanings

FAWOHODIE
"independence"

symbol of independence, freedom, emancipation

SANKOFA
"return and get it"

symbol of importance of learning from the past

GYE NYAME
"except for God"

symbol of the supremacy of God

AKOFENA
"sword of war"

ymbol of courage, valor, and heroism

BOA ME NA ME MMOA WO
"Help me and let me help you"

symbol of cooperation and interdependence

NEA ONNIM NO SUA A OHU
"He who does not know can know from learning"

symbol of knowledge, life-long education

NEA OPE SE OBEDI HENE
"he who wants to be king"

symbol of service and leadership

ADINKRAHENE
"Chief of the Adinkra symbols"

symbol of greatness, charisma and leadership

NKONSONKONSON
"chain link"

symbol of unity and human relations, that in unity lies strength

HYE WON HYE
"that which does not burn"

mbol of imperishability and endurance

ME WARE WO
"I shall marry you"

symbol of commitment, perseverance

DAME-DAME
name of a board game

symbol of intelligence and ingenuity

TIME LINE

1909 Born Francis Nwia-Kofi Nkrumah in the village of Nkroful in the Nzema area of the Gold Coast, a colony of Great Britain. In *The Autobiography of Kwame Nkrumah*, published in 1957, Nkrumah wrote that his mother said he was born in 1912 and the Catholic priest who baptized him recorded his birth as 1909. He used 1909 on official documents, he wrote, because "it was the line of least resistance."

1914 Attended a one-room school run by Catholic Missionaries where as a young student he demonstrated a gift for public speaking.

1930 Attended the Government Training School in Accra, later named Achimota College, where he also was a part-time teacher.

Became a mentee to Dr. Kwegyir Aggrey, who was the only Ghanaian teaching at the school and who was highly respected among the students.

1933 Sailed to Liverpool, England and then to the United States to attend Lincoln University. There he read widely from the writings of W.E.B. DuBois, Marcus Garvey and other Pan-Africans.

1939 Graduated from Lincoln University with a Bachelor of Arts degree and was offered a job as Assistant Lecturer in Philosophy.

Founded the African Students Association of America and Canada.

1942 Earned a Bachelor of Theology degree, a Master of Arts in Philosophy degree, and completed coursework and a preliminary exam for a Ph.D in Philosophy at the University of Pennsylvania.

Visited and spoke at many Black churches including the Abyssinian Baptist Church in Harlem where he met Rev. Adam Clayton Powell, Sr. and Rev. Adam Clayton Powell, Jr.

Also frequented the Father Jealous Divine's Peace Mission which impressed him because it provided inexpensive meals to many of Harlem's marginalized people.

1945 Left the United States and attended the Fifth Pan-African Congress in Manchester, England where he became friends with many Socialist scholars such as George Padmore, T. R. Makonnen and the South African writer Peter Abrahams.

Changed his first name to Kwame.

1946 Published his first book, *Towards Colonial Freedom.*

1947 Served as General Secretary to the United Gold Coast Convention (UGCC) and travelled throughout the Gold Coast speaking to large groups of farmers, trade unionists, market women, workers and youth.

1948 Arrested with six other members of the UGCC for his criticism of British colonialism and placed in prison in Kumasi, capital of the Ashanti Kingdom.

1949 Formed the Convention People's Party (CPP) whose slogan was "Self Government Now!"

1950 Arrested again and taken to James Fort Prison in Accra, January 22.

While imprisoned, is elected to represent CPP in the legislative government.

1951 Released on February 12 from James Fort Prison in Accra. Later met with the British governor of the Gold Coast, Sir Charles Arden-Clarke, who asked him to write a constitution to form a new parliamentary government.

1952 Became Prime Minister of the Gold Coast on March 5 after being elected to parliament.

1957 As the first Prime Minister, made his famous midnight speech on March 6th to declare the Gold Coast's independence from years of British colonial rule.

1958 Marries Helena Ritz Fathia of Egypt on New Year's Eve, 1957. Together they had three children, Sekou, Gamal and Samia Yaba.

1960 Elected president of Ghana on April 27 and given the honorary title "Osagyefo" which in the Akan language means Redeemer.

On July 1 Ghana's name officially becomes the Republic of Ghana.

1961 Sent Ghanaian troops to the Belgium Congo to support his friend Prime Minister Patrice Lumumba in that country's struggle against the Belgium colonial government.

1963 Founding member of the Organization of African Unity (OAU), which included 32 independent African states. The OAU held their conference in Addis Abba, Ethiopia.

1965 Published his book, *Neo-Colonialism: The Last Stage of Imperialism*, which is critical of the United States' and British Commonwealth's policies in Africa.

1966 On February 24, while on a peace mission in Hanoi, Viet Nam to meet with Ho Chi Minh, a military coup took place in Accra and he never again returned alive to his beloved Ghana. During his exile, from 1966-1972, he was the guest of President Ahmed Sékou Touré of Guinea who made him honorary co-president.

1972 Died on April 27 in Bucharest, Romania, after being treated there for prostate cancer.

Mortal remains are returned and buried in Accra, Ghana on July 7.

1992 Kwame Nkrumah Memorial Park and Mausoleum constructed in downtown Accra, Ghana. This national park was built on the site where Nkrumah declared Ghana's independence in the Midnight Speech of 1957.

About the Author and Illustrator

Useni Eugene Perkins is a multi-faceted writer and activist who was a prominent voice in the Black Arts Movement. His writings for young people include *Home is a Dirty Street: The Social Oppression of Black Children, Rise of the Phoenix: Voices from Chicago's Black Struggle, 1960 to 1975* (Third World Press), *Poetry from the Masters: Black Arts Movement* (Just Us Books), and a picture book, *Hey Black Child* (Little Brown) illustrated by Bryan Collier. In 1999 he was inducted into the Gwendolyn Brooks Literary Hall of Fame. In 2003 Useni was featured in HistoryMakers.com, a digital archive dedicated to preserving histories of African Americans. He has travelled to Ghana many times and in 2007 he was inducted into the Gefia Society in Akatsi, Volta Region, Ghana and was installed as their Academic Development Chief under the stool name of Torgbui Perkins Agbale I. Visit him at https://Blackchildjournal.com

Laura Freeman is the award-winning illustrator of over 30 picture books for children including *Hidden Figures: The True Story of Four Black Women and the Space Race* by Margot Lee Shetterly (Harper Collins), *Kamala Harris Rooted in Justice* by Nikki Grimes (Atheneaum) and *Dream Builders The Story of Architech Philip Freelon* by Kelly Starling Lyons (Lee and Low Books). She also illustrated six titles in the *I Love to* series (Marimba Books). A graduate of the School of Visual Arts in New York City, Laura has been awarded the Coretta Scott King Illustrator Honor and the NAACP Image Award for her work. She lives in Atlanta, GA with her husband and their two children.
Visit her at https://LFreemanArt.com

To Dr. Wolanyo Kpo and my brothers and sisters in the villages of Gefia and Tsrukpe in the Volta region of Ghana, West Africa. —U.E.P.

To the Hudsons, who took a chance on me long ago. —L.F.

Cover Design by Stephan Hudson